The Young Adult's Guide to Wealth: Breaking Free from Financial Limits

J. C.

INDEX

Introduction: Why Money Matters 6

Chapter 1: Budgeting – Your Financial Roadmap 11

Chapter 2: Saving Money – Building a Financial Cushion . 17

Chapter 3: Managing Debt - Smart Ways to Stay Out of Trouble 23

Chapter 4: Credit Scores - The Key to Unlocking Financial Opportunities 31

Chapter 5: Investing – Growing Your Wealth for the Long Term 40

Chapter 6: Building Your Investment Strategy – Tools for Long-Term Success 49

Chapter 7: Risk Management – Safeguarding Your Wealth 57

Chapter 8: Financial Independence – Building a Future of Freedom 66

Chapter 9: The Psychology of Money – How Your Mindset Shapes Your Financial Journey 76

Chapter 10: Building a Debt-Free Future – Advanced Strategies for Eliminating Debt...86

Chapter 11: Building Wealth – Turning the Page from Debt to Growth..94

Chapter 12: Financial Independence and Early Retirement (FIRE) 102

Conclusion: Taking Control of Your Financial Future ...112

Introduction: Why Money Matters

Money can seem like a complicated and intimidating subject, especially when you're just starting out in life. Many young adults feel overwhelmed by the idea of managing their finances. Maybe you've had moments where you check your bank account and wonder where all the money went. Or perhaps you've felt stressed when an unexpected expense, like a car repair or a medical bill, came up, and you didn't have the funds to cover it. It's easy to feel lost when it comes to managing money, but here's the truth: you don't need to have everything figured out from the start. Managing money isn't about being perfect or making millions overnight. It's about understanding how to make your money work for you, one step at a time.

The Importance of Financial Freedom

Money matters because it directly affects your freedom. The more control you have over your finances, the more choices you'll have in life. Whether you're saving for a dream vacation, buying your first car, or planning for something bigger like a home, understanding your finances is key to making those dreams a reality. When you know how to manage your money, you take control of your future, rather than letting your financial situation control you.

But let's make one thing clear: you don't need to be a financial expert to get started. You don't need a degree in finance or a detailed knowledge of the stock market. What you need is a willingness to learn and a few basic tools to help guide you along the way. This book is designed to do exactly that—to give you simple, actionable steps that can help you gain control of your money, no matter where you're starting from.

Take Control, One Step at a Time

Think of managing money like hiking a mountain trail. At the bottom, the peak may seem far off and intimidating. The trail is steep, winding, and filled with obstacles. But if you focus on one step at a time, the journey becomes manageable. You don't need to sprint to the top. The key is to keep moving forward, steadily, with purpose.

The same goes for your finances. Right now, it might feel like you're at the base of that mountain, looking up at a complex landscape of bills, expenses, and debts. But if you break it down into smaller, more manageable steps, you'll find that you can make real progress without feeling overwhelmed. The first step is understanding where you are. Ask yourself: How much money do I have right now? How much do I spend each week? What do I spend my money on? These simple questions form the foundation of understanding your financial situation.

Once you have a clearer picture of where your money is going, you can begin to make adjustments. Are you spending more than you're earning? Are there areas where you can cut back? These are the kinds of small but important steps that will help you take control of your finances.

Money Is About Choices, Not Sacrifices

There's a common misconception that managing money means giving up everything fun or enjoyable. People often think that if they want to save money, they have to stop going out with friends, skip the coffee shop runs, and say no to every opportunity that costs money. But that's not true. Money management isn't about deprivation; it's about making thoughtful choices.

Imagine your financial life as a pie chart. Each slice represents a different aspect of your spending: food, entertainment, rent, savings, and so on. The goal isn't to eliminate any one slice but to find a balance that allows you to enjoy your life today while still planning for your future. It's okay to spend money on things you enjoy, like going out to eat or buying a new outfit. The key is to make sure that those choices fit within your larger financial plan.

Instead of thinking of budgeting as a restriction, think of it as a tool for giving yourself more options. When you're aware of how much you're spending and where your money is going, you can make more informed decisions. Maybe that means cooking at home a few more nights a week so you can save up for a weekend getaway. Or perhaps it means setting aside a small amount each month for something you really want. Whatever your priorities, a budget helps you make room for the things that matter most to you.

The Power of Small Steps

When it comes to building good financial habits, the small things really do add up. You don't need to make drastic changes overnight. Instead, focus on making small, incremental improvements, and over time, you'll see big results.

For example, imagine setting aside just $2 a day. It might not seem like much, but over the course of a year, that's over $700 in savings. Small, consistent actions can make a significant impact, especially when it comes to money. This is the power of what's called compound interest, a concept we'll explore more in later chapters. But for now, the important thing to remember is that every little bit counts.

The same goes for cutting back on expenses. You don't need to eliminate all your fun spending, but maybe you can start by reducing unnecessary purchases. Whether that's skipping a few online impulse buys or choosing a free activity with friends instead of an expensive one, these small changes can lead to big savings over time.

Why This Book Will Help You

This book isn't about promising quick fixes or offering some secret formula for instant wealth. Instead, it's about giving you practical, straightforward advice that you can apply right away, no matter your current financial situation. Whether you're living paycheck to paycheck or have some savings set aside, the strategies in this book are designed to help you build a strong financial foundation, one step at a time.

We'll cover everything from creating a budget, to understanding debt, to making your first investments. But don't worry, you won't need any prior knowledge to follow along. Each chapter will guide you through the basics in a simple, easy-to-understand way. By the time you finish this book, you'll feel more confident about managing your money and making smart financial decisions.

The goal here isn't perfection. It's progress. As you read through each chapter, you'll learn that managing money is less about following strict rules and more about developing habits that work for you. You'll gain the tools to make informed choices, build financial stability, and ultimately create a life that gives you the freedom to pursue your goals without being held back by money worries.

So, are you ready to take that first step?

Chapter 1: Budgeting – Your Financial Roadmap

Managing your money might seem intimidating at first, but think of it like learning to drive. At the beginning, there's a lot to remember: the steering wheel, the pedals, the mirrors. But once you get the hang of it, driving becomes second nature. Budgeting is no different. It's your financial roadmap, a simple guide that helps you navigate where your money should go. If you learn the basics, you'll never feel lost when it comes to your finances. In this chapter, we'll break down how to create a budget and, more importantly, how to stick to it.

What is a Budget, and Why Do You Need One?

A budget is nothing more than a plan for your money. It helps you see how much money you have coming in (income) and how much is going out (expenses). Without a budget, it's easy to overspend, leaving you with nothing at the end of the month. Or worse, you might find yourself dipping into credit cards or loans, which can lead to debt. On the other hand, a budget gives you control. It allows you to decide in advance where your money should go, ensuring that your essential expenses are covered, your savings are growing, and you still have some left for fun.

Think of your money like a road trip. You wouldn't get in the car without a destination or map. A budget is that map. It shows you where you want to go financially and how to get there.

The 50/30/20 Rule: A Simple Way to Start

You might have heard of complex budgeting systems that require hours of tracking every penny you spend. But the truth is, you don't need to make budgeting complicated. One of the simplest and most effective ways to create a budget is the **50/30/20 rule**. Here's how it works:

- **50% on Needs**: Half of your income should go toward essential expenses—things you can't live without. This includes rent, groceries, utilities, transportation, and minimum debt payments. These are your non-negotiables, the bills you must pay to maintain your day-to-day life.

- **30% on Wants**: The next 30% is for the things that make life more enjoyable but aren't absolutely necessary. This could be dining out, buying new clothes, going to the movies, or even that daily coffee you love. These are your "wants," and it's important to remember that it's okay to spend money on things that make you happy, as long as you're mindful of how much you're spending.

- **20% on Savings and Debt**: The last 20% should be set aside for savings and paying off any outstanding debt (credit card, student loans, etc.). Building up an emergency fund, saving for retirement, or investing for your future falls under this category. This is the money that ensures you're not just living paycheck to paycheck but building a stable financial foundation.

The beauty of the 50/30/20 rule is its simplicity. It provides a clear structure while giving you the flexibility to spend money on both needs and wants, without feeling guilty. It's also a great starting point if you've never budgeted before because it's easy to remember and implement.

Tracking Your Income and Expenses

Before you can start using the 50/30/20 rule, you need to know where your money is coming from and where it's going. This might sound tedious, but tracking your income and expenses is essential to building an effective budget. Fortunately, there are plenty of tools to make this process easy.

Start by writing down all your sources of income. If you have a steady job, this is simple. But if you have multiple streams of income (like freelance work, side gigs, or tips), make sure to include those as well. Then, list all your expenses. This should include fixed expenses (rent, utilities, subscriptions) and variable expenses (groceries, transportation, dining out). The goal is to get a clear picture of your spending habits.

There are many apps available that can help you with this, such as Mint, YNAB (You Need a Budget), or even a simple spreadsheet. Once you've tracked your income and expenses for a month or two, you'll have a much better idea of where your money is going—and where you can make adjustments if necessary.

Tips for Sticking to a Budget

Creating a budget is one thing, but sticking to it is another challenge. Many people start out with good intentions, only to abandon their budget after a few weeks. The key is to find a system that works for you and your lifestyle. Here are some tips to help you stay on track:

1. **Set Realistic Goals**: Don't be overly strict with yourself. If you try to cut out all "wants" at once, you're likely to get frustrated and give up. Instead, set realistic goals for cutting back. For example, if you usually spend $100 on dining out each month, aim to reduce that to $80. Small changes are easier to stick to.

2. **Automate Your Savings**: One of the easiest ways to ensure you stick to your budget is to automate your savings. Set up a direct deposit or automatic transfer that moves a portion of your income into a savings account as soon as you get paid. This way, you don't even have to think about it, and you'll be less tempted to spend that money elsewhere.

3. **Use Cash for Discretionary Spending**: If you find it hard to control your spending, try using cash for things like entertainment, dining out, and shopping. Once the cash is gone, you know you've

reached your limit for the month. This method can make it easier to stay within your budget and avoid overspending.

4. **Review and Adjust Regularly**: A budget isn't set in stone. Life changes, and so should your budget. Maybe you get a raise, or your rent goes up, or you decide to save more for a future goal. Whatever the case, it's important to review your budget regularly and make adjustments as needed. This will keep you on track and ensure your budget is always working for you.

5. **Celebrate Small Wins**: Sticking to a budget can feel tough at times, but it's important to celebrate your progress along the way. Did you manage to save more than usual this month? Or maybe you resisted an impulse buy and put that money into your savings instead. Acknowledge these small victories—they're proof that you're moving in the right direction.

In Summary

Budgeting is the foundation of financial freedom. It's your roadmap to making informed decisions about where your money should go, ensuring you're prepared for both today and tomorrow. By using a simple system like the 50/30/20 rule, tracking your income and expenses, and making small, realistic changes, you'll not only build better financial habits but also gain the confidence to take control of your money—and your future.

Remember, a budget is not a restriction. It's a tool that gives you the freedom to live the life you want, without constantly worrying about money. So, take that first step, set up your budget, and start feeling empowered about your financial journey.

Chapter 2: Saving Money – Building a Financial Cushion

Saving money is often easier said than done. Many of us have the best intentions of saving, but when the end of the month rolls around, we're left wondering where all our money went. The key to saving effectively isn't about depriving yourself of the things you enjoy; it's about developing habits that allow you to grow your savings without feeling like you're constantly sacrificing your lifestyle. In this chapter, we'll explore practical strategies to build a financial cushion, why saving is so important, and how to make it a seamless part of your life.

Pay Yourself First: The Golden Rule of Saving

One of the most powerful ways to save money is by following a simple principle: **pay yourself first**. What does that mean? It means before you spend a single dollar on bills, groceries, or entertainment, you set aside money for yourself. Think of saving as the most important "bill" you pay each month.

Most people treat saving as something they do with whatever money is left at the end of the month—if there's anything left. This approach rarely works because, let's be honest, there's always something to spend money on. But when you prioritize saving and do it first, you guarantee that you're building a cushion for the future.

Here's how to implement this strategy: as soon as you receive your paycheck, set aside a specific percentage or dollar amount for your savings. Even if you start small —say 5-10%—the act of consistently putting money into savings first will make a huge difference over time.

Emergency Funds: Why You Need One and How to Build It

Life is unpredictable, and unexpected expenses are bound to come up. Whether it's a car repair, a medical bill, or an emergency flight to visit family, having an emergency fund can save you from financial stress and keep you from going into debt. An emergency fund is a savings account specifically for life's "what if" moments, and it should be one of your top financial priorities.

Why is an emergency fund so important?

Without one, you might have to rely on credit cards or loans when unexpected costs arise, which can lead to more debt and financial instability. Having a financial buffer allows you to handle these situations without panicking or derailing your long-term financial goals.

How much should you save in an emergency fund?

A good rule of thumb is to aim for three to six months' worth of living expenses. This might sound overwhelming at first, especially if you're just starting to save, but don't worry—it's not about reaching that goal overnight. Start small. Set a short-term goal to save $500 or $1,000. Once you hit that, gradually work toward your bigger goal of having several months of expenses covered.

Where should you keep your emergency fund?

Your emergency fund should be easily accessible but not so easy that you'll be tempted to dip into it for non-emergencies. A high-yield savings account is a great option because it offers more interest than a regular savings account while keeping your money safe and accessible when you need it.

Easy Ways to Start Saving More

Saving money doesn't have to be painful or restrictive. There are plenty of small changes you can make that will allow you to save more without drastically changing your lifestyle. Here are some practical tips to help you get started:

1. **Automate Your Savings**: One of the easiest ways to save more is to automate the process. Set up an automatic transfer from your checking account to your savings account every time you get paid. This way, you don't have to rely on willpower to save money—it happens automatically, without you even thinking about it.

2. **Round-Up Savings**: Some banks and apps offer a feature that rounds up your purchases to the nearest dollar and deposits the difference into your savings account. For example, if you spend $4.25 on coffee, the app will round that up to $5 and move $0.75 to savings. It's an effortless way to save without feeling it.

3. **Save Windfalls**: Anytime you receive unexpected money—whether it's a tax refund, a birthday gift, or a bonus at work—consider putting a portion, if not all, of it directly into savings. Since this money wasn't part of your regular budget, you won't miss it, but it can make a big difference in your savings account.

4. **Cut One Small Expense**: Look at your regular spending and find one small expense that you can cut or reduce. Maybe it's a streaming service you rarely use or those takeout meals that add up each week. Even cutting a $10 or $20 expense and putting that money into savings can add up to hundreds of dollars over the course of a year.

5. **Save Spare Change**: If you use cash often, make it a habit to save your spare change at the end of each day. You'd be surprised how quickly it adds up. Once the jar is full, take it to the bank and deposit it into your savings account.

Automating Your Savings: Making It Effortless

Automation is one of the best tools in your financial toolkit. When it comes to saving, the less effort required, the better. As mentioned earlier, setting up an automatic transfer to your savings account is a great way to ensure you're consistently saving, even if you forget or get too busy.

You can automate your savings in several ways:

- **Direct Deposit**: Some employers allow you to split your paycheck so that a portion goes directly into your savings account. This way, you never even see the money in your checking account, making it less tempting to spend.
- **Savings Apps**: Many apps can help you automate your savings. Apps like Acorns, Digit, or Qapital offer creative ways to save by rounding up purchases, analyzing your spending patterns, and transferring small amounts to savings.

The goal is to make saving money as effortless as possible. When it becomes automatic, you'll be saving without even thinking about it, and over time, that small effort will grow into a significant financial cushion.

In Summary

Saving money is one of the most important financial habits you can develop. Whether you're building an emergency fund, saving for a big purchase, or putting money aside for the future, saving allows you to create financial stability and security. By paying yourself first, building an emergency fund, and automating your savings, you'll set yourself up for financial success without feeling like you're constantly sacrificing.

Remember, you don't have to save large amounts all at once. Start small, and let those small efforts build over time. With consistency and patience, you'll be surprised by how quickly your savings grow, giving you more financial freedom and peace of mind.

Chapter 3: Managing Debt - Smart Ways to Stay Out of Trouble

Debt is one of those things that, when managed properly, can be a useful tool. But when left unchecked, it can quickly spiral out of control, dragging you into a cycle of stress, anxiety, and financial instability. Whether it's student loans, credit cards, or other forms of borrowing, understanding how to manage debt is crucial for maintaining a healthy financial life.

In this chapter, we'll break down the different types of debt, how to manage them wisely, and strategies for paying off debt faster. Most importantly, you'll learn how to avoid getting into trouble with debt in the first place.

Understanding Good Debt vs. Bad Debt

Not all debt is created equal. While the idea of being debt-free sounds appealing, there are certain types of debt that can actually help you build wealth in the long run. The key is knowing the difference between good debt and bad debt.

Good debt refers to money borrowed for things that have the potential to increase your wealth or improve your financial situation over time. The classic example is student loans. When used wisely, student loans allow you to invest in your education, which can lead to better job opportunities and higher earning potential.

Similarly, a mortgage is often considered good debt because it allows you to purchase a home, an asset that can appreciate in value over time.

Even some business loans can be good debt if they help you start or expand a business that generates more income.

The important thing to remember about good debt is that it's typically low-interest and tied to an asset that appreciates or generates income. You're borrowing money to make more money in the long run, and you have a clear plan to pay it back.

Bad debt, on the other hand, refers to borrowing money to purchase things that lose value or don't provide any financial return. The biggest culprit? Credit card debt. Credit cards often come with high interest rates, and using them to buy things like clothes, electronics, or vacations can lead to a cycle of borrowing and repayment that's hard to escape.

Another example of bad debt is taking out loans for depreciating assets, like a car loan. While having a car might be necessary, cars lose value over time, meaning you're paying interest on something that's worth less and less as the years go by.

The key takeaway? Not all debt is bad, but you should be careful about taking on debt that doesn't serve a long-term purpose or that has high interest rates. Good debt should be viewed as an investment in your future, while bad debt should be avoided or paid off as quickly as possible.

The Dangers of Credit Card Debt

Credit cards can be useful tools if you know how to use them responsibly. They offer convenience, and many come with rewards like cashback or travel points. But they also come with a hidden danger: high interest rates. If you're not careful, credit card debt can balloon out of control, especially if you only make the minimum payments each month.

How Credit Card Interest Works

Credit card interest is calculated based on your Annual Percentage Rate (APR), which is the amount of interest you'll pay on any balance that you don't pay off in full by the due date. If you carry a balance from month to month, the interest compounds, meaning you'll be charged interest on top of interest.

For example, if you have a $1,000 balance with an APR of 18%, and you only make the minimum payment each month, it could take years to pay off that debt—and you could end up paying hundreds or even thousands of dollars in interest along the way.

The Minimum Payment Trap

Making only the minimum payment is one of the biggest traps when it comes to credit card debt. While it might seem like a manageable way to pay off your balance, in reality, you're barely covering the interest each month, which means your balance will stay high and take much longer to pay off.

To avoid falling into this trap, aim to pay off your balance in full each month. If that's not possible, try to pay as much as you can above the minimum payment. The more you pay, the less interest you'll accumulate, and the faster you'll be debt-free.

How to Pay Off Debt: Snowball vs. Avalanche Method

If you've accumulated debt and want to pay it off efficiently, there are two popular strategies to consider: the Snowball Method and the Avalanche Method. Each has its advantages, and the best approach depends on your financial situation and personality.

The Snowball Method

The Snowball Method focuses on paying off your debts from smallest to largest, regardless of interest rates. Here's how it works:

1. List all your debts from smallest to largest balance.

2. Make the minimum payment on all your debts, except for the smallest one.
3. Put any extra money toward paying off the smallest debt.
4. Once the smallest debt is paid off, move on to the next smallest debt, and repeat.

The Snowball Method works well because it gives you quick wins early on. As you pay off smaller debts, you'll feel a sense of accomplishment, which can motivate you to keep going. It's a great option if you need a psychological boost to stay on track with debt repayment.

The Avalanche Method

The Avalanche Method, on the other hand, focuses on paying off debts with the highest interest rates first. Here's how it works:

- List all your debts from highest to lowest interest rate.
- Make the minimum payment on all your debts, except for the one with the highest interest rate.
- Put any extra money toward paying off the highest-interest debt.
- Once that debt is paid off, move on to the next highest interest rate, and repeat.

The Avalanche Method is the most cost-effective way to pay off debt because it minimizes the amount of interest you'll pay over time. However, it might take longer to see progress if your highest-interest debt is also your largest balance. This method is ideal if you're more concerned with saving money on interest than with seeing quick wins.

Avoiding Debt in the Future

The best way to manage debt is to avoid it whenever possible. Here are some strategies to help you steer clear of debt and maintain financial stability:

A. Live Within Your Means: One of the most important rules of personal finance is to spend less than you earn. If you're consistently relying on credit cards or loans to cover basic expenses, it's a sign that you need to reevaluate your spending habits and create a more sustainable budget.

B. Save for Large Purchases: Instead of using credit to buy expensive items, make it a goal to save up for them in advance. Whether it's a new phone, a vacation, or a car, having the cash on hand will keep you from taking on unnecessary debt.

C. Build an Emergency Fund: As we discussed in the previous chapter, having an emergency fund is crucial for avoiding debt. When unexpected expenses arise, you can tap into your savings instead of relying on credit cards or loans.

D. Use Credit Responsibly: If you do use credit cards, treat them like a debit card. Only charge what you can afford to pay off in full each month. This will help you build a good credit score without accumulating debt.

E. Avoid High-Interest Loans: Be cautious about taking out loans with high interest rates, such as payday loans or cash advances. These types of loans can trap you in a cycle of debt that's difficult to escape. If you need to borrow money, look for lower-interest options, such as personal loans or a line of credit from a bank.

In Summary

Debt can be a powerful financial tool, but it can also be a major source of stress if not managed properly. By understanding the difference between good and bad debt, using credit cards responsibly, and choosing a debt repayment strategy that works for you, you can avoid the pitfalls of debt and stay in control of your financial future.

Whether you choose the Snowball Method or the Avalanche Method, the key is consistency and commitment. And remember, avoiding unnecessary debt in the first place by living within your means, saving for large purchases, and building an emergency fund is the best way to stay financially stable in the long run.

Debt doesn't have to be scary. With the right approach, you can manage it wisely, pay it off efficiently, and avoid falling into the same traps in the future. In the next chapter, we'll explore one of the most important aspects of personal finance—your credit score, and how it can impact your financial life for years to come.

Chapter 4: Credit Scores - The Key to Unlocking Financial Opportunities

Your credit score is one of the most important numbers in your financial life. Whether you're applying for a loan, renting an apartment, or even getting a job, your credit score can have a huge impact on the opportunities available to you. Yet, for many young adults, credit scores remain a mystery—something abstract and difficult to understand.

In this chapter, we'll break down what a credit score is, how it's calculated, why it matters, and most importantly, how to improve and maintain a good score. Understanding your credit score will give you more control over your financial future and open doors to better opportunities, like lower interest rates, better credit terms, and more financial flexibility.

What Is a Credit Score?

Your credit score is a three-digit number that represents your creditworthiness—essentially, how trustworthy you are when it comes to repaying borrowed money. It's like a financial report card that lenders, landlords, and even some employers use to assess your risk.

The most common type of credit score is the FICO score, which ranges from 300 to 850. The higher your score, the better your creditworthiness. Here's a general breakdown of what the different ranges mean:

I. *800-850 (Excellent):* You're in the top tier of credit scores. With a score in this range, you'll have access to the best interest rates and terms on loans and credit cards.

II. *740-799 (Very Good):* You're still in great shape and can expect competitive rates and favorable terms on most types of credit.

III. *670-739 (Good):* You have a solid credit score that qualifies you for most credit products, though you may not get the absolute best rates.

IV. *580-669 (Fair):* You might still qualify for credit, but you'll likely face higher interest rates and less favorable terms.

V. *300-579 (Poor):* Your credit score is considered risky, making it difficult to qualify for credit, and if you do, you'll face steep interest rates and limited options.

While a poor credit score can make life more difficult, the good news is that your credit score is not fixed. It can change over time, and with the right habits, you can improve it significantly.

How Is Your Credit Score Calculated?

To understand how to improve your credit score, it's important to know how it's calculated. While the exact formula used by credit reporting agencies is proprietary, there are five major factors that influence your score:

- Payment History (35%): This is the most important factor in your credit score. Lenders want to know if you pay your bills on time. Late or missed payments, especially those that are 30 days or more past due, can seriously hurt your score. On the flip side, consistently paying your bills on time will help boost your score over time.

- Amounts Owed (30%): This factor looks at how much you owe in relation to your available credit. If you're using most of your available credit (for example, if your credit card balances are close to the limit), it signals to lenders that you might be overextended, which can hurt your score. Ideally, you should aim to keep your credit utilization ratio—the percentage of your total available credit that you're using—below 30%.

- Length of Credit History (15%): The longer you've been using credit, the better. Lenders like to see a long track record of responsible credit use. This is why it's often recommended to keep your oldest credit card accounts open, even if you don't use them frequently, because they help establish a longer credit history.

- New Credit (10%): Opening too many new credit accounts in a short period of time can be a red flag for lenders, as it might suggest that you're in financial trouble. Every time you apply for credit, a hard inquiry is made on your credit report, which can temporarily

lower your score. Try to space out credit applications and only apply for new credit when you really need it.
- Credit Mix (10%): Lenders like to see that you can manage different types of credit responsibly. This includes a mix of installment loans (like student loans or car loans) and revolving credit (like credit cards). Having a diverse credit portfolio can help improve your score, but it's not as critical as the other factors.

Why Your Credit Score Matters

Your credit score might seem like just a number, but it has a real impact on your life. Here are a few key reasons why your credit score matters:

1. Access to Credit and Loans - When you apply for a credit card, a car loan, or a mortgage, your credit score is one of the first things lenders look at. A higher score makes you more likely to be approved and gives you access to lower interest rates. Lower interest rates can save you thousands of dollars over the life of a loan. For example, imagine you're taking out a $200,000 mortgage. With a credit score in the excellent range, you might qualify for an interest rate of 3%, while someone with a fair score might get a rate of 5%. That difference in interest rates could mean paying tens of thousands of dollars more over the course of the loan.
2. Renting an Apartment - Many landlords check credit scores before approving a rental application. A low

credit score can make it harder to rent an apartment, and even if you're approved, you might be required to pay a larger security deposit or have a co-signer. A high credit score, on the other hand, can make the rental process smoother and give you more options.

3. Employment Opportunities - Some employers, especially for jobs in finance or positions that require security clearances, may check your credit report as part of the hiring process. While they won't see your exact credit score, they'll be able to see if you have a history of late payments, collections, or other red flags. A solid credit history can enhance your job prospects, especially in industries where financial responsibility is important.

4. Insurance Premiums - Believe it or not, your credit score can also affect your insurance premiums. Some insurance companies use credit-based insurance scores to determine how much you'll pay for auto or home insurance. A lower score could result in higher premiums, while a higher score can save you money on your insurance bills.

How to Improve Your Credit Score

If your credit score isn't where you want it to be, don't worry. There are several steps you can take to improve it over time. Here are some of the most effective strategies:

- **Pay Your Bills on Time** - Since payment history is the largest factor in your credit score, consistently paying your bills on time is the most important thing you can do to improve it. Set up reminders or automatic payments to ensure you don't miss any due dates.

- **Reduce Your Credit Card Balances** - High credit card balances relative to your credit limits can hurt your score, so aim to pay down your balances and keep your credit utilization below 30%. If possible, pay your credit card balances in full each month to avoid interest charges and improve your score.

- **Avoid Closing Old Accounts** - As mentioned earlier, the length of your credit history matters. Even if you don't use an old credit card anymore, keeping the account open can help boost your score by increasing the average age of your credit accounts. Just be sure that there are no annual fees on the card, and if there are, weigh the costs of keeping it open against the benefits.

- **Be Strategic About New Credit** - While it might be tempting to open a new credit card for a sign-up bonus or a store discount, applying for too much credit in a short period can hurt your score. Be selective about when and where you apply for new credit. Each hard inquiry on your credit report lowers your score slightly, so avoid unnecessary credit checks.

- **Check Your Credit Report Regularly** - Errors on your credit report can drag your score down without you even knowing it. That's why it's important to check your credit report at least once a year to make sure everything is accurate. You're entitled to a free credit report from each of the three major credit bureaus (Equifax, Experian, and TransUnion) once a year through AnnualCreditReport.com. If you notice any mistakes, such as accounts you didn't open or late payments that you actually made on time, dispute them with the credit bureau to have them corrected. Correcting errors can provide an immediate boost to your credit score.

- **Use a Secured Credit Card** - If you're just starting out or trying to rebuild your credit after a rough patch, a secured credit card can be a useful tool. Secured cards require a cash deposit, which acts as your credit limit. Using a secured card responsibly—by making small purchases and paying them off in full each month—can help you establish or rebuild a positive credit history.

How Long Does It Take to Improve Your Credit Score?

Improving your credit score doesn't happen overnight, but with patience and consistency, you can see significant improvements within a few months. The exact timeline depends on your starting point and the actions you take. If you're starting from scratch or recovering from serious issues like late payments or collections, it might take longer to see substantial progress. However, small changes, such as reducing credit card balances or disputing errors on your credit report, can have a quicker impact.

It's important to remember that your credit score is a long-term game. The habits you build today—paying bills on time, using credit responsibly, and avoiding unnecessary debt—will pay off in the long run.

The Importance of Credit Monitoring

As you work on improving your credit score, consider signing up for credit monitoring services. These services alert you to changes in your credit report, such as new accounts being opened or changes to your balances. While there are paid options, many credit card companies and financial institutions offer free credit monitoring tools. This is a great way to keep an eye on your progress and catch potential issues, such as identity theft, early.

In Summary

Your credit score is one of the most important financial tools you have, affecting everything from your ability to rent an apartment to the interest rates you get on loans. A good credit score opens doors to financial opportunities, while a poor score can limit your options and cost you more in the long run.

The good news is that your credit score is within your control. By understanding the factors that affect your score and taking proactive steps to improve it—like paying your bills on time, keeping credit card balances low, and checking your credit report regularly—you can build and maintain a strong credit score.

Remember, building good credit takes time, but the rewards are worth the effort. With a solid credit score, you'll have more financial flexibility, lower interest rates, and greater peace of mind. As we continue on this journey through personal finance, we'll dive into another critical aspect of financial stability: investing. In the next chapter, we'll explore how to start investing and why it's one of the best ways to grow your wealth over time.

Chapter 5: Investing – Growing Your Wealth for the Long Term

Investing might seem like a complicated or even intimidating concept at first. For many young adults, the world of stocks, bonds, and mutual funds can feel overwhelming, with jargon like "diversification," "capital gains," and "index funds" making it seem like investing is only for wealthy or highly experienced individuals. But the truth is, investing is one of the most powerful ways to grow your wealth over time, and it's accessible to everyone, no matter your current income or financial knowledge.

In this chapter, we'll break down the basics of investing in a way that's easy to understand. You'll learn why investing is essential for long-term financial growth, how to get started, and the different types of investments you can make. The goal is to empower you to take control of your financial future by making your money work for you.

Why Invest?

You might wonder, "Why should I invest when I can just save my money in a bank account?" While saving is important, there's a fundamental difference between **saving** and **investing**.

Saving is setting aside money for short-term needs, emergencies, or specific goals, often in a savings account. While this is a safe and necessary part of managing your finances, it typically offers low returns, especially when interest rates are low.

Investing, on the other hand, is putting your money into assets like stocks, bonds, or real estate, with the expectation that they will grow in value over time. While investing comes with more risk than saving, it also has the potential to offer much higher returns in the long run.

The primary reason to invest is to build wealth over time. Historically, the stock market has provided an average annual return of around 7-10% after inflation. While there are ups and downs along the way, investing allows your money to grow faster than it would in a typical savings account. This is especially important when you consider inflation, which reduces the purchasing power of your money over time. If your money isn't growing, it's actually losing value.

Another key reason to invest is to reach long-term goals. Whether you're planning for retirement, saving for a home, or building a college fund, investing can help you achieve those big financial milestones faster than saving alone.

The Power of Compound Interest

One of the most powerful tools in investing is compound interest. When you invest, your money earns a return, and then that return starts to earn more returns. Over time, this compounding effect can turn even small investments into significant sums.

Let's break it down with an example: imagine you invest $1,000 in a stock that earns an average annual return of 8%. After one year, you'll have $1,080. In the second year, you'll earn 8% not just on your original $1,000, but on the $1,080. This process repeats year after year, with your investment growing faster as the returns compound.

The earlier you start investing, the more time your money has to compound, which is why time is one of the most important factors in successful investing. Even if you can only invest a small amount now, starting early gives you a significant advantage in the long run.

How to Get Started with Investing

Getting started with investing is easier than ever. Thanks to the rise of online brokerage accounts and robo-advisors, you don't need a lot of money or advanced knowledge to begin. Here's a step-by-step guide to help you start investing:

1. Set Clear Goals

Before you start investing, it's important to know what you're investing for. Are you building a retirement fund? Saving for a down payment on a house? Trying to build wealth for general financial security? Your goals will help determine the types of investments that are best for you and the time horizon you should consider.

For example:

- If you're investing for a long-term goal like retirement, you might choose a more aggressive strategy, focusing on stocks that offer higher potential returns.

- If you're investing for a shorter-term goal (like buying a house in five years), you might want a more conservative approach, with a focus on bonds or safer assets that offer lower risk.

2. Choose an Investment Account

To start investing, you'll need an investment account. The two main types of accounts for beginners are:

- Brokerage Account: This is a regular investment account where you can buy and sell stocks, bonds, mutual funds, and other assets. Brokerage accounts are flexible, but any profits you make are subject to taxes.

- Retirement Account (IRA or 401(k)): These accounts offer tax advantages for long-term saving. With an IRA (Individual Retirement Account) or a 401(k) (typically offered by employers), you can invest for retirement with tax-deferred or tax-free growth. However, there are penalties for withdrawing funds before a certain age.

Many online brokers, like Fidelity, Vanguard, and Robinhood, offer low-cost brokerage accounts that are easy to open and manage. Robo-advisors like Betterment and Wealthfront are another great option for beginners, as they automate the investment process by creating a portfolio tailored to your goals and risk tolerance.

3. *Decide How Much to Invest*

One of the biggest misconceptions about investing is that you need a lot of money to get started. The truth is, you can start with as little as $50 or $100. The key is to invest consistently over time.

A good rule of thumb is to invest 10-15% of your income if possible. If that's too much for you right now, start with whatever you can afford and gradually increase the amount over time.

4. Choose Your Investments

Once you've opened an account and decided how much to invest, the next step is to choose your investments. There are several types of investments to consider, each with its own level of risk and return potential:

- Stocks: When you buy a stock, you're purchasing a share of ownership in a company. Stocks offer the highest potential returns but also come with the most risk, as their value can fluctuate greatly in the short term. Over the long term, however, stocks have historically provided strong returns.

- Bonds: Bonds are loans that you give to a company or government in exchange for regular interest payments and the return of your principal when the bond matures. Bonds are generally considered safer than stocks, but they offer lower returns.

- Mutual Funds: Mutual funds pool money from many investors to buy a diversified portfolio of stocks, bonds, or other assets. They offer diversification, which reduces risk, but they come with fees that can eat into your returns over time.

- Exchange-Traded Funds (ETFs): ETFs are similar to mutual funds but trade like stocks. They often have lower fees than mutual funds and are a popular choice for beginner investors.

- Index Funds: These are a type of mutual fund or ETF that tracks a specific market index, like the S&P 500. Index funds are a great option for beginners because they offer broad market exposure, low fees, and consistent returns over time.

For most beginners, a diversified mix of stocks and bonds, often through index funds or ETFs, is a smart and simple way to start.

5. *Understand Risk and Reward*

Investing always involves some level of risk. The value of your investments can go up or down, especially in the short term. However, over the long term, investing in a diversified portfolio of assets has historically been a reliable way to grow wealth.

It's important to understand your risk tolerance—how much risk you're comfortable taking. Younger investors with a longer time horizon can afford to take more risks because they have time to ride out market fluctuations. Older investors or those with shorter-term goals may want to take a more conservative approach.

6. Be Patient and Stay Consistent

One of the biggest mistakes new investors make is trying to time the market—buying when prices are low and selling when they're high. The truth is, no one can predict the market with certainty, and trying to do so can lead to poor decisions and missed opportunities.

The best approach to investing is to stay consistent. Invest regularly, whether the market is up or down, and avoid making impulsive decisions based on short-term market movements. Over time, the market tends to go up, and the longer you stay invested, the more you'll benefit from compound growth.

The Importance of Diversification

One of the most important principles of investing is diversification—the practice of spreading your investments across different asset classes, industries, and regions to reduce risk. Think of it as not putting all your eggs in one basket.

For example, if you invest all your money in the stock of one company and that company goes bankrupt, you could lose everything. But if you invest in a mix of different stocks, bonds, and funds, a downturn in one area is less likely to hurt your overall portfolio.

Diversification doesn't guarantee profits, but it can help smooth out the ups and downs of the market and protect you from major losses.

In Summary

Investing is one of the most effective ways to build wealth and achieve long-term financial goals. While it may seem complex at first, it's easier than ever to get started, and the earlier you begin, the more time your money has to grow.

By understanding the basics—setting clear goals, choosing the right accounts and investments, and staying patient—you can build a strong investment portfolio that grows with you over time. In the next chapter, we'll dive deeper into specific investment strategies, such as dollar-cost averaging, retirement planning, and managing risk, so you can feel confident on your investing journey.

Chapter 6: Building Your Investment Strategy – Tools for Long-Term Success

Now that you have a solid understanding of what investing is and why it's so important, it's time to dive into investment strategies. These strategies are essentially roadmaps for how to invest your money in a way that aligns with your goals, risk tolerance, and timeline.

Whether you're investing for retirement, saving for a home, or just trying to grow your wealth, having a clear strategy in place is key to staying on track and making smart financial decisions. In this chapter, we'll explore some of the most common and effective strategies for growing your investments over time.

1. Dollar-Cost Averaging: Investing Consistently Over Time

One of the simplest and most effective investment strategies is called dollar-cost averaging. It's a fancy term for a simple concept: investing a fixed amount of money at regular intervals, regardless of the market's ups and downs.

Let's break it down. With dollar-cost averaging, instead of trying to time the market by buying low and selling high (which is extremely difficult to do consistently), you commit to investing a set amount of money on a regular basis—say, $100 every month. This way, you're buying more shares when prices are low and fewer shares when prices are high. Over time, this can lower the average cost of your investments and help smooth out the volatility of the market.

For example, if you're investing in an index fund that fluctuates in price, here's what dollar-cost averaging might look like:

- Month 1: The price of the fund is $50 per share, so your $100 buys you 2 shares.

- Month 2: The price drops to $40 per share, so your $100 buys you 2.5 shares.

- Month 3: The price goes up to $60 per share, so your $100 buys you 1.67 shares.

At the end of three months, you've spent $300 and own a total of 6.17 shares. Your average cost per share is about $48.60—not bad, considering the fund hit a high of $60.

The beauty of dollar-cost averaging is that it takes the emotion out of investing. Instead of worrying about whether now is the right time to invest, you stick to a plan, knowing that over the long term, the market tends to rise. This approach also encourages discipline—you're investing regularly, which is one of the most important habits to build.

2. The 60/40 Rule: Balancing Risk and Reward

Another popular investment strategy is the 60/40 rule, which involves allocating 60% of your investment portfolio to stocks and 40% to bonds. This strategy is designed to strike a balance between risk and reward. Stocks typically offer higher returns but come with more volatility, while bonds are generally safer but offer lower returns.

Here's how it works:

- 60% in stocks: Stocks provide the growth potential. While they can fluctuate in the short term, they historically provide solid returns over the long term, making them essential for growing your wealth.

- 40% in bonds: Bonds help protect your portfolio from the volatility of the stock market. They provide more stable, albeit smaller, returns and can act as a buffer during market downturns.

This strategy is often used by investors who want to grow their wealth while minimizing risk. However, it's important to note that the 60/40 split isn't set in stone. Some younger investors, for example, might choose a more aggressive mix, such as 80% in stocks and 20% in bonds, since they have more time to recover from potential losses.

As you get closer to reaching your financial goals—such as retirement or buying a house—you might want to shift your allocation to include more bonds and fewer stocks to protect the wealth you've accumulated.

3. Investing for Retirement: The Power of Tax-Advantaged Accounts

Retirement might seem like a long way off, but investing for retirement is one of the most important financial decisions you can make. The earlier you start, the easier it will be to build a comfortable nest egg for your future.

One of the best ways to invest for retirement is through tax-advantaged accounts, like an IRA (Individual Retirement Account) or a 401(k). These accounts offer significant tax benefits that can help your money grow faster. Let's take a closer look at these options:

Traditional IRA and 401(k)

- Tax-deferred growth: With a traditional IRA or 401(k), the money you contribute is tax-deductible, meaning you don't pay taxes on it now. Instead, your investments grow tax-deferred, and you only pay taxes when you withdraw the money in retirement.

- Employer matching (401(k)): If your employer offers a 401(k) match, take full advantage of it. This is essentially free money—your employer is contributing to your retirement fund, and it can significantly boost your savings over time.

Roth IRA and Roth 401(k)

- Tax-free growth: With a Roth IRA or Roth 401(k), you contribute after-tax dollars, meaning you don't get a tax deduction now. However, your investments grow tax-free, and you won't owe any taxes when you withdraw the money in retirement. This can be a huge advantage, especially if you expect to be in a higher tax bracket when you retire.

The key to successful retirement investing is consistency and patience. By contributing regularly to your retirement accounts, you can take advantage of compound growth and build a solid financial foundation for your future.

4. Rebalancing Your Portfolio: Staying on Track

As you invest over time, the value of your stocks and bonds will change, which can throw your portfolio's allocation out of balance. For example, if the stock market performs well, your 60/40 mix might shift to 70% stocks and 30% bonds. While this might seem like a good problem to have, it's important to rebalance your portfolio periodically to maintain your desired level of risk.

Rebalancing simply means adjusting your portfolio by selling assets that have grown too large and buying assets that have become underrepresented. In the example above, you would sell some stocks and buy more bonds to bring your allocation back to 60/40.

Many investors rebalance their portfolios once or twice a year. Some brokerage accounts and robo-advisors even offer automatic rebalancing, so you don't have to worry about doing it yourself.

5. Investing in Index Funds: A Simple, Low-Cost Approach

If you're looking for a simple and low-cost way to invest, index funds are a great option. Index funds are a type of mutual fund or ETF that track a specific market index, like the S&P 500. By investing in an index fund, you're essentially buying a small piece of every company in that index, giving you broad exposure to the market.

Why are index funds so popular? Here are a few reasons:

- Low fees: Index funds typically have lower fees than actively managed funds, because they don't require a team of analysts to pick stocks. Over time, lower fees can significantly boost your returns.

- Diversification: Since index funds invest in many companies, they offer instant diversification, which helps reduce risk.

- Consistent performance: While index funds won't outperform the market, they also won't underperform it. Over the long term, the stock market tends to rise, so an index fund that tracks the market can provide reliable returns.

For most investors, a mix of index funds that cover different parts of the market (such as U.S. stocks, international stocks, and bonds) is a simple, effective way to build a diversified portfolio.

6. Staying the Course: Avoid Emotional Investing

One of the biggest challenges in investing is staying disciplined, especially when the market is volatile. It can be tempting to sell when prices drop or chase hot stocks when prices are rising. But emotional investing is one of the biggest pitfalls for new investors.

Remember: Investing is a long-term game. The stock market has ups and downs, but over the long term, it tends to go up. Trying to time the market or make decisions based on short-term emotions can hurt your returns.

Instead, stick to your investment strategy. Keep contributing regularly, rebalance when necessary, and avoid making impulsive decisions based on market news or short-term movements. The best investors are those who stay patient and let their money grow over time.

In Summary

Building a successful investment strategy is all about setting clear goals, staying disciplined, and making smart choices with your money. Whether you're using dollar-cost averaging, the 60/40 rule, or investing in index funds, the key is to stay consistent and think long term.

In the next chapter, we'll explore how to protect your investments and wealth by understanding risk management, including how to avoid common investing mistakes and how to prepare for market downturns.

Chapter 7: Risk Management – Safeguarding Your Wealth

Investing can be an exciting way to build your financial future, but it's important to remember that with any opportunity for reward, there comes an element of risk. Managing risk effectively is essential to long-term success, and understanding how to protect your investments is just as important as knowing how to grow them.

In this chapter, we'll explore how to manage the risks that come with investing, avoid common mistakes, and prepare yourself for the inevitable ups and downs of the market. The goal is not to avoid risk entirely, but to understand it and learn how to minimize it in a way that supports your long-term financial goals.

1. Understanding Different Types of Risk

When it comes to investing, the word "risk" can mean different things depending on the situation. Let's break down some of the most common types of risk you'll encounter:

- Market Risk: This is the risk that the overall stock market will decline. When the market falls, most stocks tend to follow, regardless of the company's specific performance. Market risk is often driven by economic events, political instability, or shifts in investor sentiment.

- Company-Specific Risk: This is the risk that a particular company will underperform or even fail. If you invest in a single stock, your entire investment is tied to that one company's success. Company-specific risk is why diversification is so important.

- Inflation Risk: Inflation slowly reduces the purchasing power of your money over time. If the return on your investments doesn't outpace inflation, your money loses value in real terms. This is why investing in assets like stocks, which historically offer returns that beat inflation, is crucial for long-term growth.

- Interest Rate Risk: Changes in interest rates can affect the value of certain investments, especially bonds. When interest rates rise, bond prices usually fall, and vice versa. This risk is more relevant if you invest in fixed-income securities.

- Liquidity Risk: Liquidity refers to how easily you can buy or sell an investment. Some assets, like real estate or certain bonds, may take longer to sell without taking a loss. Stocks and ETFs, on the other hand, are usually highly liquid, meaning they can be sold quickly if needed.

By understanding these risks, you can better prepare yourself and your portfolio to navigate them.

2. Diversification: Your Best Defense Against Risk

Diversification is one of the most powerful tools in your risk management arsenal. It's the process of spreading your investments across different asset classes, industries, and even geographic regions to reduce the impact of any single investment's poor performance.

Think of diversification as the old saying: *Don't put all your eggs in one basket*. By spreading your investments out, you lower the chances that a downturn in one area will sink your entire portfolio.

Here's how you can diversify your investments:

- Across Asset Classes: Don't invest solely in stocks or bonds. A balanced portfolio might include stocks for growth, bonds for stability, and other assets like real estate or commodities for further diversification.

- Within Asset Classes: Even if you're heavily invested in stocks, you can diversify by investing in different sectors (like technology, healthcare, and consumer goods) and different regions (such as the U.S., Europe, and emerging markets).

- Use Funds for Instant Diversification: Mutual funds and ETFs are great tools for diversification because they allow you to invest in many different companies or bonds with a single purchase. An index fund that tracks the S&P 500, for example, gives you exposure to 500 different companies in one investment.

3. Risk Tolerance: Knowing How Much Risk You Can Handle

Not everyone has the same capacity for risk. Your risk tolerance is a personal measure of how much volatility and uncertainty you're willing to endure in your investments. It's influenced by a variety of factors, including:

- Time Horizon: How long you plan to keep your money invested plays a big role in your risk tolerance. If you're investing for a goal that's 30 years away, you can afford to take more risk because you have time to recover from any market downturns. If your goal is only five years away, you'll want to invest more conservatively.

- Financial Situation: If you have a stable income and a solid emergency fund, you may feel more comfortable taking on risk than someone with a less secure financial situation.

- Emotional Comfort: Risk tolerance is also about how well you can handle the stress of market fluctuations. Some people can ride out a 20% drop in the stock market without batting an eye, while others might panic and sell everything. Understanding your emotional relationship with risk can help you create a portfolio that won't keep you up at night.

Assessing your risk tolerance will help guide your asset allocation. If you're more risk-averse, you might opt for a higher percentage of bonds and a lower percentage of stocks. If you can handle more risk, you might lean more heavily into stocks, which have higher potential returns but greater short-term volatility.

4. Building an Emergency Fund: Your Safety Net

Before you start taking on significant investment risk, it's crucial to have an emergency fund in place. An emergency fund is a stash of money set aside to cover unexpected expenses, such as medical bills, car repairs, or temporary unemployment.

Why is an emergency fund important for risk management? It prevents you from having to dip into your investments during a market downturn. If you don't have cash set aside and an emergency strikes, you may be forced to sell investments at a loss to cover your expenses. This can seriously derail your long-term financial goals.

A good rule of thumb is to have three to six months' worth of living expenses saved in a high-yield savings account. Once your emergency fund is fully funded, you can invest more confidently, knowing that your short-term needs are covered.

5. The Importance of Staying Calm During Market Volatility

The stock market doesn't go up in a straight line—it's normal for prices to fluctuate. However, market downturns can trigger fear and anxiety, leading some investors to make rash decisions that hurt them in the long run.

Here's what you should do during periods of market volatility:

- Stay the Course: Remember that investing is a long-term game. Market corrections and bear markets are normal, and historically, the market has always recovered from downturns. The worst thing you can do is sell everything in a panic. By staying invested, you give yourself the opportunity to benefit from the eventual recovery.

- Avoid Emotional Decisions: Making investment decisions based on emotions is a recipe for disaster. When the market is down, it can be tempting to sell to avoid further losses. But by doing so, you're locking in those losses and missing out on the potential for gains when the market rebounds.

- Reassess, Don't React: If you're feeling anxious during a market downturn, it might be a sign that your asset allocation doesn't match your risk tolerance. Take the time to reassess your portfolio and make adjustments, but avoid making knee-jerk reactions based on short-term market movements.

6. Avoiding Common Investment Mistakes

Even experienced investors make mistakes from time to time. But by being aware of some of the most common pitfalls, you can avoid costly errors and keep your investment strategy on track. Here are a few mistakes to watch out for:

- Chasing Performance: It's easy to get caught up in the hype of a hot stock or sector, but chasing past performance is rarely a winning strategy. By the time an investment has gained a lot of attention, much of its potential upside may already be priced in. Stick to your long-term strategy instead of chasing short-term trends.

- Not Diversifying Enough: Putting all your money into one or two investments can lead to significant losses if those investments underperform. Make sure your portfolio is diversified across different asset classes and sectors to reduce risk.

- Trying to Time the Market: Timing the market—buying low and selling high—sounds great in theory, but it's nearly impossible to do consistently. Many investors who try to time the market end up missing out on gains because they sell too soon or wait too long to buy back in. Instead, focus on staying invested and sticking to your plan.

- Ignoring Fees: Investment fees might seem small, but over time they can significantly eat into your returns. Be mindful of the fees associated with your investments, and opt for low-cost index funds or ETFs when possible.

7. Insurance: Protecting Your Investments from Catastrophe

While diversification and long-term thinking can protect you from many risks, there are some events that can pose significant financial risks outside the stock market. This is where insurance comes in. Having the right insurance policies in place can protect you from catastrophic financial losses that could wipe out your investments.

Consider the following types of insurance:

- Health Insurance: Medical expenses are one of the leading causes of bankruptcy. Having adequate health insurance can protect you from devastating medical bills.

- Disability Insurance: This protects your income in case you're unable to work due to illness or injury. If you rely on your income to support your investment goals, disability insurance can be crucial.

- Home and Auto Insurance: Protecting your home and car from accidents, natural disasters, and theft is essential. Without the right coverage, you could face significant financial losses.

In Summary

Managing risk is a fundamental part of any successful investment strategy. By diversifying your portfolio, staying calm during market downturns, avoiding common mistakes, and having an emergency fund and insurance in place, you can protect your investments and ensure that you're on the path to long-term financial success.

In the next chapter, we'll explore the concept of financial independence and how you can use the power of investing to build a life where money works for you.

Chapter 8: Financial Independence – Building a Future of Freedom

Financial independence is more than just a catchy phrase—it's a lifestyle, a mindset, and a goal that can radically transform how you think about money. At its core, financial independence (often shortened to FI) means having enough wealth and passive income to cover your living expenses without relying on a traditional job.

For many people, the idea of not having to work for money is both exciting and daunting. It's not about getting rich quickly or retiring tomorrow, but about freedom—the freedom to choose how you spend your time and energy. Whether you want to retire early, travel the world, start a passion project, or just have peace of mind, financial independence can help you get there.

In this chapter, we'll explore what it takes to achieve financial independence, the key strategies to get you there, and how you can start building a life where money works for you.

1. What is Financial Independence?

Financial independence is the point where your passive income (income that doesn't require active work) covers all your expenses. In other words, you're no longer dependent on a paycheck to live your life. For most people, the journey to financial independence involves building a combination of investments, savings, and other income streams that grow and generate returns over time.

Let's break it down further:

- Passive Income: This includes income from sources like dividends, interest from savings and bonds, rental income, and capital gains from investments. The goal is to have these income streams be large enough to cover your living expenses.

- Financial Independence Ratio: Some people aim for their financial independence ratio to be 100%. This ratio is calculated by dividing your passive income by your living expenses. For example, if you need $40,000 a year to live comfortably and your investments generate $40,000 a year in passive income, your ratio is 100%, meaning you've achieved financial independence.

Financial independence doesn't necessarily mean you have to stop working; it just means you have the freedom to work on what you want, when you want, without worrying about money.

2. Why Strive for Financial Independence?

The reasons for pursuing financial independence vary from person to person, but here are a few common motivations:

- Freedom to Choose: FI gives you the freedom to decide how to spend your time. Whether it's pursuing a passion project, traveling, or simply spending more time with family, you're no longer tied to a job just to pay the bills.

- Security and Peace of Mind: Reaching financial independence means you're less vulnerable to financial emergencies or job loss. You have a safety net that allows you to weather economic storms with less stress.

- Flexibility in Life Choices: Financial independence gives you the flexibility to make bold life changes—like starting your own business, taking a sabbatical, or pursuing a different career—without the fear of financial instability.

- Early Retirement: While not everyone pursuing FI wants to retire early, many do. Achieving financial independence can allow you to retire in your 40s, 30s, or even earlier if you're dedicated to the journey.

3. The FIRE Movement – Financial Independence, Retire Early

You may have heard of the FIRE movement, which stands for Financial Independence, Retire Early. This movement has gained popularity in recent years as more people seek to gain control over their finances and live life on their own terms. The FIRE community is diverse, with some people aiming to retire as early as their 30s or 40s, while others simply want the option to work less or pursue passion projects.

There are different approaches to FIRE, including:

- Lean FIRE: Achieving financial independence with a more minimalist lifestyle, where you live on less and save more aggressively.

- Fat FIRE: Achieving financial independence but with a higher standard of living, allowing for more luxuries and comforts in your budget.

- Barista FIRE: Achieving a level of financial independence where you can cover most of your expenses with passive income, but still work a part-time job or side hustle to supplement your income. This approach gives you more flexibility while still enjoying the benefits of FI.

No matter which version of FIRE appeals to you, the goal remains the same: building wealth and passive income streams that allow you to live life on your own terms.

4. How to Achieve Financial Independence

Achieving financial independence requires discipline, planning, and smart decision-making. Here are the core strategies to help you get there:

A. Live Below Your Means

This is one of the most important principles in the FI journey. The more you save, the faster you can reach financial independence. Living below your means means spending less than you earn and putting the difference to work by investing and saving.

- Track Your Spending: Start by tracking where your money is going. You can't improve what you don't measure, so knowing exactly how much you're spending each month will help you identify areas where you can cut back.

- Reduce Lifestyle Inflation: As your income increases, it's tempting to increase your spending (a nicer car, a bigger house, more vacations). But if you can resist lifestyle inflation and continue living like you're earning less, you'll be able to save and invest more aggressively.

B. Save and Invest Aggressively

Saving is essential, but it's not enough on its own—you need to invest your money so it grows over time. The power of compound interest means that your money can grow exponentially if given enough time. Here's how to approach saving and investing for FI:

- Set a High Savings Rate: Many people in the FI community aim for a savings rate of 50% or more of their income. While this might not be possible for everyone, the more you can save, the faster you'll reach financial independence.

- Invest in Low-Cost Index Funds: As we discussed in earlier chapters, index funds are a great way to invest in the stock market with low fees and broad diversification. By consistently investing in a diversified portfolio, you can grow your wealth over time.

- Max Out Tax-Advantaged Accounts: Take advantage of tax-advantaged accounts like IRAs, 401(k)s, or Roth IRAs to maximize your savings. These accounts offer tax benefits that can help your money grow faster.

C. Focus on Increasing Income

While cutting expenses is important, increasing your income can accelerate your path to financial independence. Here are a few ways to boost your earnings:

- Negotiate Your Salary: If you're in a salaried position, don't be afraid to negotiate for raises. Earning more each year means you can save and invest more.

- Start a Side Hustle: Many people pursuing FI supplement their income with side businesses or freelance work. Whether it's starting a blog, freelancing online, or creating a small business, a side hustle can provide extra income that goes directly into your savings and investments.

- Invest in Yourself: Building skills and expanding your knowledge can lead to higher-paying opportunities. Whether it's taking a course, getting a certification, or learning new skills, investing in yourself can have a huge payoff.

D. Minimize Debt and Manage It Wisely

Debt can be a major obstacle on the road to financial independence, especially high-interest debt like credit cards or personal loans. Here's how to approach debt:

- Pay Off High-Interest Debt First: If you have credit card debt or personal loans with high interest rates, prioritize paying these off as quickly as possible. The interest on these debts can eat away at your savings and investments.

- Use Debt Strategically: Not all debt is bad—mortgages and student loans, for example, can be useful for building wealth over the long term. The key is to manage debt wisely and ensure that it doesn't prevent you from saving and investing.

E. Automate Your Savings and Investments

Automating your finances can take the stress out of saving and investing. By setting up automatic transfers to your savings accounts and investment portfolios, you can ensure that you're consistently making progress toward financial independence without having to think about it.

5. The 4% Rule: How Much Do You Need to Be Financially Independent?

One of the most common questions on the road to financial independence is, "How much money do I need?" A popular rule of thumb is the 4% rule, which suggests that you can withdraw 4% of your investment portfolio each year in retirement without running out of money.

Here's how it works:

- To calculate how much you need to achieve FI, multiply your annual expenses by 25. For example, if you need $40,000 a year to live comfortably, you'd need a portfolio of $1,000,000 ($40,000 x 25) to retire.

The 4% rule is based on historical market data and assumes that your portfolio is invested in a diversified mix of stocks and bonds. While it's not a perfect rule, it provides a helpful benchmark for setting your financial independence target.

6. The Emotional Side of Financial Independence

While the numbers and strategies are important, the journey to financial independence is also a deeply emotional one. It requires discipline, patience, and a willingness to make sacrifices in the short term for the sake of long-term freedom.

- Delayed Gratification: One of the hardest parts of pursuing FI is learning to delay gratification. While your friends might be spending on fancy vacations or new cars, you're focused on saving and investing. But remember, the sacrifices you make today are setting you up for a future of freedom and choice.

- Enjoy the Journey: Achieving FI takes time, and it's important to enjoy the journey along the way. While saving aggressively is key, don't forget to live your life and find happiness in the present. Financial independence is about creating options for your future, not depriving yourself of joy in the present.

In Summary

Financial independence is a powerful goal that can transform how you approach money, work, and life. By living below your means, saving and investing aggressively, and staying focused on your long-term goals, you can build a future where money works for you, not the other way around.

In the next chapter, we'll dive into the psychology of money and how your mindset can make or break your financial journey.

Chapter 9: The Psychology of Money – How Your Mindset Shapes Your Financial Journey

When we think of managing money, we often focus on numbers—income, expenses, savings rates, and investment returns. But there's a deeper, less tangible force at play in our financial lives: our mindset. The way we think, feel, and react to money can shape our financial future just as much as the concrete steps we take to manage it.

Understanding the psychology of money is critical because it helps us recognize the emotional and mental habits that influence our financial decisions. Whether you're aiming for financial independence or simply trying to stay out of debt, mastering your mindset is key to lasting financial success.

In this chapter, we'll explore the most common psychological biases and habits that can either help or hinder your financial progress. By understanding and addressing these, you can become more aware of how your emotions and beliefs about money shape your decisions—and how to make better choices as a result.

1. The Emotional Side of Money

Money is not just a means of exchange; it's deeply intertwined with our emotions. For some, it represents security and stability. For others, it's a source of stress, fear, or even shame. These emotional connections can stem from childhood experiences, cultural influences, and even the way we see ourselves.

Fear and Anxiety

Many people feel anxious when thinking about money— whether it's the fear of not having enough, the pressure to save, or the constant worry about bills. This fear can lead to avoidance behaviors, such as putting off budgeting, avoiding financial conversations, or delaying important decisions like investing.

- Avoidance Trap: Some people avoid dealing with their finances because the emotions tied to money feel overwhelming. They might not open bank statements, fail to track expenses, or procrastinate on financial planning because the thought of confronting their financial situation feels too uncomfortable.

To counteract this, it's essential to start small. Begin by setting aside just a few minutes each week to look at your finances. The more you engage with your money, the less power those fears and anxieties will have over you.

Impulse Spending and Instant Gratification

On the opposite end of the spectrum, some people use money to deal with negative emotions, such as stress, boredom, or sadness. This often manifests as impulse spending—buying things on a whim, not because they're necessary, but because they provide a temporary emotional boost.

Impulse spending is often linked to the need for instant gratification, the desire to experience pleasure or relief immediately rather than waiting for long-term rewards. In today's world of one-click shopping and social media ads, it's easier than ever to fall into this trap.

- The Emotional High: Impulse purchases can give us a quick emotional high, but the satisfaction is usually short-lived. After the initial excitement wears off, we're left with regret, guilt, or even stress from overspending.

Combatting this requires mindfulness—being aware of your emotions when you're making spending decisions. Before making a purchase, ask yourself if it's driven by a real need or an emotional impulse. If it's the latter, give yourself time to cool off before making a decision.

2. Cognitive Biases and How They Affect Financial Decisions

Cognitive biases are mental shortcuts that can lead us to make irrational or suboptimal decisions. These biases can have a significant impact on our financial lives, often without us even realizing it. Let's explore some of the most common biases and how they influence the way we handle money.

Loss Aversion

People tend to fear losses more than they value gains, a phenomenon known as loss aversion. In other words, losing $100 feels more painful than gaining $100 feels good. This bias can prevent us from taking risks that could be beneficial in the long run, such as investing in the stock market or starting a new business.

- Over-Cautious Investing: Due to loss aversion, some people shy away from investing in stocks or other assets that involve risk. While it's true that investments can lose value, staying too conservative—by keeping all your money in cash or low-yield savings accounts—can prevent you from growing your wealth and reaching your financial goals.

Overcoming loss aversion requires reframing how we think about risk. Instead of focusing solely on potential losses, consider the long-term benefits of investing and the risks of not investing (such as inflation eroding your savings).

The Sunk Cost Fallacy

The sunk cost fallacy is the tendency to continue investing time, money, or energy into something simply because you've already invested in it, even when it no longer makes sense to do so. This bias often shows up in financial decisions like holding onto losing investments or continuing to pay for a service you no longer use.

- Examples: Staying invested in a failing stock because you've already put a lot of money into it, or continuing to subscribe to an expensive service you rarely use because you feel bad about "wasting" the money.

To avoid this, recognize that the money you've already spent (a sunk cost) is gone, and making decisions based on future benefits is the best way to move forward. Ask yourself, "If I were starting fresh, would I make this decision again?"

Anchoring

Anchoring occurs when we rely too heavily on the first piece of information we encounter when making decisions. For example, when you see a $200 jacket marked down to $100, the original price of $200 becomes the "anchor," making $100 seem like a great deal—even if $100 is still more than you would normally spend.

- Retail Trick: Stores often use anchoring to make sales prices seem more attractive, even when the discounted price is still high. Understanding this bias can help you become more critical of deals and avoid spending more than you intended.

Anchoring can also affect our savings goals. If you set a target savings amount based on a random number you've heard (such as "you need $1 million to retire"), you may anchor your decisions on that number without fully considering your unique circumstances.

Confirmation Bias

Confirmation bias is the tendency to seek out information that confirms what we already believe while ignoring or dismissing evidence that contradicts our views. In the context of money, this can lead to poor decision-making, as we selectively pay attention to information that reinforces our current financial habits or beliefs.

- Example: If you believe that a particular stock is going to perform well, you might only read articles that support that belief while ignoring warnings or signs that it could underperform.

To combat confirmation bias, make a habit of seeking out diverse opinions and challenging your assumptions. This will help you make more balanced, informed financial decisions.

3. The Importance of a Growth Mindset

One of the most powerful tools for financial success is a growth mindset—the belief that you can improve, learn, and grow over time. People with a growth mindset see challenges as opportunities for growth and are more likely to take positive steps toward improving their financial situation.

On the other hand, people with a fixed mindset believe their abilities are set in stone and are less likely to try new strategies or take risks because they fear failure.

- How It Affects Money: If you have a fixed mindset, you might believe that you're just "bad with money" or that "financial success isn't for people like me." This can lead to a sense of defeat or helplessness when it comes to managing your finances.

Cultivating a growth mindset can help you view financial mistakes as learning opportunities rather than personal failures. Whether it's paying off debt, saving for a big goal, or learning to invest, a growth mindset will help you stay motivated and resilient through setbacks.

4. Rewriting Your Money Story

Everyone has a "money story"—the beliefs and attitudes about money that shape how they handle their finances. These stories often stem from childhood experiences, family dynamics, and cultural norms. While some people have positive money stories that empower them to make good financial decisions, others may have negative stories that hold them back.

Common Negative Money Stories

- "I'm not good with money."
- "I'll never get out of debt."
- "Money is the root of all evil."
- "I'll never be able to afford the life I want."

These stories can become self-fulfilling prophecies if left unchecked. The good news is that you can rewrite your money story. By becoming aware of the negative beliefs that hold you back and replacing them with positive, empowering beliefs, you can change the way you approach money.

- New Money Stories: "I'm learning to manage my money better every day." "I have the power to change my financial situation." "Money is a tool that I can use to create freedom."

5. Practical Steps to Improve Your Money Mindset

Improving your money mindset doesn't happen overnight, but with consistent effort, you can make significant progress. Here are a few practical steps to start shifting your mindset:

- Practice Gratitude: Focus on what you have, rather than what you lack. Gratitude can help reduce feelings of scarcity and increase feelings of abundance.

- Set Positive Financial Goals: Instead of focusing on what you want to avoid (e.g., "I don't want to be in debt"), focus on what you want to achieve (e.g., "I want to build an emergency fund").

- Surround Yourself with Positive Influences: The people you surround yourself with can greatly influence your financial mindset. Seek out friends, mentors, or online communities that support your financial goals and encourage positive habits.

- Educate Yourself: Financial literacy is key to building confidence in your money decisions. The more you learn about budgeting, investing, and saving, the more empowered you'll feel to take control of your financial future.

In Summary

The psychology of money plays a huge role in how we manage our finances. By becoming aware of the emotions, biases, and beliefs that shape your financial decisions, you can start making more intentional choices and build a healthier relationship with money. With a growth mindset and a willingness to rewrite your money story, you can set yourself up for long-term success.

In the next chapter, we'll look at debt management strategies—how to get out of debt and use debt wisely to build a better financial future.

Chapter 10: Building a Debt-Free Future – Advanced Strategies for Eliminating Debt

By now, you understand the different types of debt and have been introduced to basic repayment strategies. But becoming debt-free isn't just about paying off balances — it's about building a sustainable lifestyle that prevents debt from creeping back in and finding ways to use debt strategically, only when it benefits your long-term goals. In this chapter, we'll explore advanced strategies for eliminating debt, preventing future debt, and reshaping your financial habits to build a more secure future.

1. Breaking the Debt Cycle

One of the most challenging aspects of debt is the cycle that often traps people. You pay off one loan, but another pops up—whether it's an emergency expense, a tempting offer to upgrade your lifestyle, or a sudden life change. Breaking this cycle requires more than just financial tools; it requires a shift in your financial behavior and mindset.

Create a Debt Prevention Plan

Preventing future debt begins with having a concrete, actionable plan to avoid situations where debt becomes a necessity. This means building a strong emergency fund, living below your means, and identifying potential debt traps before they arise.

- Build an Emergency Fund: This is your first line of defense against future debt. A fund that covers three to six months of living expenses ensures that when unexpected expenses arise, you won't need to rely on credit cards or loans.

- Adopt a "Cash-First" Mentality: To break free from the reliance on credit, start adopting a mentality where, as much as possible, you pay for things in cash (or with a debit card) instead of credit. If you don't have the cash available for a purchase, it's often a sign to reassess whether it's truly necessary.

- Plan for Large Expenses: Whether it's replacing your car, funding education, or taking a vacation, large expenses are a part of life. Rather than turning to debt, plan ahead by saving a portion of your income each month toward these goals.

Eliminate Temptations

Debt is often tied to lifestyle inflation, the tendency to spend more as your income increases. As you make more money, the pressure to upgrade your car, home, or wardrobe grows. But this constant push to "level up" financially often leads to taking on more debt to maintain a lifestyle that's beyond your means.

- Declutter Your Financial Life: Unsubscribe from marketing emails, avoid shopping apps, and eliminate browsing social media accounts that encourage spending. The less exposure you have to temptations, the easier it is to stay focused on your financial goals.

- Learn to Say "No": One of the hardest parts of breaking the debt cycle is learning to say no—to yourself, to others, and to society's expectations. By practicing the art of saying no, especially when it comes to things that don't align with your priorities, you give yourself the freedom to live within your means and stay debt-free.

2. Advanced Debt Repayment Techniques

Once you've got the basics down, it's time to accelerate your debt repayment efforts with more advanced techniques. These approaches go beyond simple budgeting and focus on aggressive strategies to help you wipe out debt faster.

The Extra Payment Strategy

One of the most powerful ways to speed up your debt repayment is by making extra payments on top of your regular monthly payments. Every extra dollar you put toward your debt goes directly to paying off the principal, reducing the overall interest you'll pay over time.

- Round Up Your Payments: Whenever possible, round up your debt payments to the nearest $50 or $100. This small adjustment can make a big difference over time, as those extra payments will reduce the principal more quickly and cut down on interest costs. For example, if your minimum monthly payment is $175, round it up to $200 or even $250. This seemingly small change can shorten your repayment timeline significantly.

- Use Windfalls to Your Advantage: Any time you receive unexpected money—whether it's a tax refund, bonus, gift, or side hustle income—put a portion (or all) of it toward your debt. This strategy accelerates your progress and allows you to avoid lifestyle inflation, where extra income leads to more spending rather than financial improvement.

Biweekly Payments

Instead of making monthly payments, consider switching to biweekly payments. This involves splitting your regular monthly payment in half and paying that amount every two weeks. Over the course of a year, you'll make the equivalent of one extra monthly payment, as there are 26 biweekly periods, but only 12 months. This approach helps you chip away at your debt faster without significantly altering your budget.

- Set up automatic biweekly payments if your lender allows it, or manually pay half of your monthly debt obligation every two weeks. This small change can shorten your debt term and save you a substantial amount in interest.

Negotiating with Creditors

It's often overlooked, but you can negotiate with your creditors to reduce interest rates, waive fees, or even lower your debt. Many lenders are willing to negotiate, especially if you've been making consistent payments or have a good credit history.

- Request Lower Interest Rates: Call your credit card companies and lenders and ask if they can reduce your interest rate. If you have a good payment history, they might be willing to lower your rate to keep you as a customer. This can significantly reduce the total amount you'll pay over time.

- Debt Settlement: If you're struggling to keep up with payments, consider working with a debt settlement company or negotiating directly with your lender. In some cases, creditors may agree to accept a lump sum payment for less than what you owe, especially if they believe it's better than receiving nothing at all. Keep in mind that this approach can negatively impact your credit score, so use it only as a last resort.

3. Reshaping Your Relationship with Debt

Once you've made significant progress in eliminating your debt, it's crucial to shift your mindset about borrowing money. Having a healthy relationship with debt doesn't mean avoiding it at all costs but understanding when it can be used strategically and when to stay away.

Only Use Debt as Leverage

Debt can be a useful tool when it's used as leverage to build wealth or achieve long-term financial goals. However, before taking on any new debt, it's essential to ask yourself if this debt will improve your financial position or if it's simply delaying a financial strain.

- Debt for Investments: If you're considering taking on debt to invest in real estate, a business, or education, carefully weigh the potential returns against the costs. Debt can be powerful when it's tied to assets that appreciate over time or improve your earning potential.

- Avoid Debt for Consumer Spending: On the other hand, debt used to finance depreciating assets—like cars, clothes, or gadgets—should generally be avoided. These purchases may bring short-term satisfaction, but they can set you back financially in the long run.

Monitor Your Credit Regularly

Even after becoming debt-free, maintaining a healthy credit score is essential. Regularly monitoring your credit ensures you stay informed about your financial health and can help you catch any errors or signs of identity theft early.

- Use Free Credit Monitoring Tools: Many services offer free credit monitoring, alerting you to any changes in your credit report. By staying on top of your credit score, you can catch problems early and ensure that your debt-free status is reflected positively.

- Focus on Responsible Credit Usage: After paying off your debt, it's important to use credit responsibly. Keep credit card balances low, pay off the full balance each month, and avoid opening too many new accounts. This will help you maintain a strong credit score and avoid falling back into debt.

4. Rewarding Yourself for Success

Eliminating debt is a major financial milestone, and it's important to celebrate your success along the way. Rewarding yourself doesn't mean spending recklessly—it means acknowledging the progress you've made and staying motivated to continue building financial health.

Set Milestone Rewards

When you pay off a significant amount of debt or clear an entire loan, give yourself permission to celebrate with a small, planned reward. This could be something like a nice dinner, a weekend getaway, or an experience you've been saving for.

- Budget for Fun: Once you've built a sustainable budget and become debt-free, it's important to strike a balance between saving and enjoying your life. Setting aside money for fun or non-essential purchases helps prevent burnout and ensures you're living a balanced financial life.

In Summary

Becoming debt-free is about more than just making payments—it's about breaking the cycle, adopting new habits, and reshaping your relationship with debt for the long term. By using advanced repayment strategies, being mindful of your future borrowing decisions, and rewarding yourself for your hard work, you can build a financial future that's not only debt-free but thriving.

In the next chapter, we'll discuss building wealth, where you can finally shift your focus from paying off debt to growing your assets and creating a secure financial future.

Chapter 11: Building Wealth – Turning the Page from Debt to Growth

Now that you've conquered debt, the next phase of your financial journey is wealth building. This chapter is all about taking the tools, habits, and discipline you've developed and shifting them toward growing your wealth and securing your financial future. Building wealth is more than just saving money—it's about making smart decisions that allow your money to work for you.

In this chapter, we'll explore ways to grow your financial assets, make your income more productive, and create a long-term plan that allows you to achieve financial independence.

1. The Power of Compound Growth

One of the most fundamental concepts in wealth building is compound interest. This is the idea that your investments earn returns not just on the original amount you invested, but also on the interest that accumulates over time. The earlier you start investing, the more time your money has to grow, even with relatively modest contributions.

Starting Early

Time is one of the most powerful factors when it comes to building wealth. The longer your money is invested, the more it can grow. Even small amounts invested consistently over time can lead to substantial wealth thanks to the effects of compound growth.

For example, let's say you invest $5,000 per year starting at age 25 with an average return of 7%. By the time you're 65, your investment will have grown to over $1 million. Compare that to someone who starts investing the same amount per year at age 35—they would end up with around $500,000 by age 65. Starting earlier gives your money more time to grow exponentially.

Consistent Contributions

Building wealth isn't about one-time investments; it's about consistent, long-term contributions. Regularly putting money into your savings and investments—whether through automatic transfers or a disciplined saving strategy—ensures that you're always growing your financial foundation.

One useful strategy is to automate your investments. Many platforms and banks allow you to set up automatic transfers from your checking account to an investment account. This way, you don't have to think about it—you're steadily building wealth without any extra effort.

2. Investing Wisely

Investing is a cornerstone of wealth building. While there are many ways to invest, the key is to choose a strategy that matches your goals, risk tolerance, and timeline. Investing wisely doesn't mean timing the market or chasing hot trends—it's about sticking to a plan that aligns with your financial future.

Diversification

One of the most important principles in investing is diversification. This means spreading your investments across different types of assets—stocks, bonds, real estate, and other opportunities—so that your portfolio isn't overly reliant on one investment type. Diversifying reduces risk because it ensures that a downturn in one market won't devastate your entire portfolio.

- Stocks: These are shares of ownership in a company. Over the long term, stocks have historically provided the highest returns, but they can also be volatile in the short term.

- Bonds: Bonds are essentially loans to a company or government, and they pay regular interest over a set period. While bonds typically provide lower returns than stocks, they are also considered safer, especially for short- to medium-term goals.

- Real Estate: Investing in property, whether through buying real estate directly or through real estate investment trusts (REITs), can provide diversification and generate rental income or appreciate in value over time.

- Other Investments: Depending on your risk tolerance, you might also consider alternative investments like commodities, cryptocurrencies, or private equity. However, these are generally riskier and should only be a small portion of a diversified portfolio.

Low-Cost Index Funds

For most individual investors, low-cost index funds are an excellent way to build wealth without having to manage the complexities of individual stock picking. Index funds are designed to track the performance of a specific market index (such as the S&P 500), which means they give you broad exposure to a wide range of companies.

The benefit of index funds is that they provide diversification at a very low cost. Instead of paying high fees for active management, index funds have minimal fees, allowing more of your money to stay invested and grow over time. They also tend to outperform most actively managed funds over the long term.

3. Boosting Your Income

Wealth building isn't just about saving and investing; it's also about maximizing your income. By increasing your income, you can accelerate your financial progress and have more money to invest and save for the future. While boosting your income may seem difficult, there are several strategies you can explore.

Side Hustles

One of the most popular ways to increase your income is through a side hustle. A side hustle is any type of job or business you take on outside of your regular work to generate extra income. With the rise of the gig economy and digital platforms, there are more opportunities than ever to earn extra money through freelance work, online businesses, or part-time gigs.

- Freelancing: If you have a skill like writing, design, coding, or marketing, freelancing platforms like Upwork, Fiverr, or Freelancer allow you to offer your services to a global audience.

- Online Business: You can create an online business by selling products through platforms like Etsy, eBay, or Amazon. Alternatively, you might offer digital products or courses if you have expertise in a specific area.

Negotiating Your Salary

If you're employed, negotiating your salary is one of the most effective ways to increase your income. Many people leave money on the table simply because they don't ask for a raise or negotiate a better starting salary. Doing research on industry standards and being prepared to make a compelling case for your value can lead to significant increases in income over time.

4. Minimizing Taxes

Taxes are one of the biggest expenses you'll face over your lifetime, so minimizing your tax burden is crucial to wealth building. While paying taxes is unavoidable, there are strategies to reduce the amount you owe and keep more of your hard-earned money.

Maximizing Tax-Advantaged Accounts

One of the most effective ways to minimize taxes is to take full advantage of tax-advantaged accounts, such as 401(k)s, IRAs, and Health Savings Accounts (HSAs). Contributions to these accounts are often tax-deductible or tax-deferred, meaning you can reduce your taxable income while growing your investments.

- 401(k) Plans: Many employers offer 401(k) plans, which allow you to save for retirement while deferring taxes on your contributions until you withdraw the money in retirement. Some employers even match contributions, giving you free money toward your retirement.

- IRAs: An Individual Retirement Account (IRA) offers similar benefits to a 401(k) but is typically available to individuals without an employer-sponsored retirement plan. Traditional IRAs offer tax-deferred growth, while Roth IRAs offer tax-free withdrawals in retirement.

- HSAs: If you have a high-deductible health plan, an HSA allows you to save money for medical expenses tax-free. Contributions, earnings, and withdrawals for qualified medical expenses are all tax-free, making it a powerful tool for minimizing taxes and covering healthcare costs.

Tax-Efficient Investments

Choosing tax-efficient investments can also help reduce your tax burden. Some investments, like municipal bonds, generate tax-free income, while others, like stocks held for the long term, are subject to lower capital gains taxes. It's important to structure your investments in a way that maximizes after-tax returns, not just pre-tax returns.

In Summary

Building wealth is about making smart, long-term financial decisions that grow your money over time. By leveraging compound interest, investing wisely, increasing your income, and minimizing taxes, you can take control of your financial future and work toward financial independence.

In the next chapter, we'll dive into financial independence and early retirement (FIRE), exploring how you can accelerate your wealth-building efforts and create a life where you no longer need to work for money but let your money work for you.

Chapter 12: Financial Independence and Early Retirement (FIRE)

As you progress through your financial journey, the concept of Financial Independence, Retire Early (FIRE) becomes an enticing goal. FIRE is not just about accumulating wealth, but about designing a life that offers you the freedom to choose how you spend your time, free from financial constraints. In this chapter, we'll explore the principles behind achieving financial independence and how early retirement can become a reality for those who are willing to commit to a disciplined, strategic approach.

1. What is FIRE?

FIRE is a movement that emphasizes aggressive saving and investing with the goal of achieving financial independence well before the traditional retirement age. The idea is to save and invest a significant portion of your income—typically 50% or more—so that you can live off the returns of your investments, freeing yourself from the need to work.

There are different variations of FIRE, depending on your financial goals and desired lifestyle:

- Lean FIRE: This approach involves living a very frugal lifestyle to retire with a smaller amount of money. It's ideal for those who prefer simplicity and are willing to make significant lifestyle changes to achieve financial freedom sooner.

- Fat FIRE: This version of FIRE allows for a more comfortable or even luxurious retirement by accumulating a larger nest egg. It's for those who want financial independence but without sacrificing their current standard of living.

- Barista FIRE: A middle ground where you save enough to cover most of your living expenses through investments but continue to work part-time to cover any additional needs. This version offers more flexibility without the need to fully retire.

2. Calculating Your FIRE Number

To achieve financial independence, you need to determine your FIRE number, the amount of money required to retire early and live off your investments. This is typically calculated based on your annual expenses and the 4% rule, a widely used principle that suggests you can safely withdraw 4% of your investment portfolio annually without running out of money.

Here's how to calculate your FIRE number:

1. Estimate Your Annual Expenses: Start by calculating how much you'll need each year in retirement. This

includes housing, food, healthcare, entertainment, travel, and any other regular expenses. Remember, your expenses may decrease in retirement if you downsize your living situation, no longer commute, or cut back on discretionary spending.

2. Multiply by 25: According to the 4% rule, you can multiply your annual expenses by 25 to determine how much you need to retire. For example, if you estimate that you'll need $40,000 per year, you would need a portfolio of $1,000,000 ($40,000 x 25).

3. Adjust for Inflation: It's important to account for inflation when calculating your FIRE number. Over time, the cost of living will increase, so ensure that your calculations allow for future expenses, not just current ones.

3. Aggressive Saving and Frugality

One of the core tenets of FIRE is aggressive saving. To retire early, you must save a much higher percentage of your income than the traditional 10-15%. Most FIRE followers aim to save 50% or more of their income, which requires a commitment to living well below your means and practicing extreme frugality.

Cutting Expenses

The key to achieving aggressive saving is to cut expenses wherever possible without sacrificing your quality of life more than you're comfortable with. This involves looking critically at your spending habits and finding ways to reduce your outflow.

Here are some strategies to consider:

- Housing: Housing is usually the biggest expense for most people. Consider downsizing to a smaller home, moving to a less expensive area, or even adopting alternative living arrangements, such as house hacking, where you rent out part of your home to cover your mortgage or rent.

- Transportation: Instead of financing a new car, opt for a reliable used vehicle that you can pay for in cash. Additionally, use public transportation, bike, or walk when possible to save on gas and maintenance costs.

- Food: Plan meals in advance, cook at home, and avoid eating out frequently. Bulk buying, couponing, and choosing cheaper food options can significantly reduce your grocery bill.

- Entertainment: Instead of spending money on expensive outings or subscriptions, look for free or low-cost entertainment options like hiking, reading, or local community events. Cutting cable, limiting streaming services, and reducing impulse purchases can also save a lot over time.

Boosting Income

While cutting expenses is one side of the FIRE equation, the other is increasing your income. The more money you bring in, the more you can save and invest toward your FIRE goals.

Consider these options:

- Side Hustles: As mentioned in earlier chapters, a side hustle can help you bring in extra income. The key is to find something that's sustainable and doesn't detract from your full-time work. Freelancing, teaching online courses, or even renting out a room or property can provide additional cash flow.

- Career Growth: Focusing on growing your main income stream is crucial. Seek promotions, ask for raises, or transition into higher-paying roles. Upskilling through certifications or additional education can help you advance in your career and increase your earning potential.

- Entrepreneurship: Starting a business or passive income streams, like creating a blog, investing in rental properties, or writing a book, can provide a source of income that grows independently of your time.

4. Investing for FIRE

Investing is the engine that drives the FIRE movement. Simply saving money in a bank account won't provide the growth you need to achieve financial independence. Instead, you must focus on investing in vehicles that provide strong long-term returns.

Index Funds

For most FIRE adherents, low-cost index funds are the backbone of their investment strategy. These funds provide broad market exposure, are relatively low risk compared to individual stock picking, and have historically provided returns of around 7-10% per year. Index funds are a hands-off way to grow your portfolio without the need to constantly monitor or adjust your investments.

Real Estate

Investing in real estate can provide both income (through rental properties) and long-term appreciation. Many FIRE advocates choose real estate as part of their wealth-building strategy because it can generate a steady stream of passive income. Whether through owning rental properties, investing in real estate investment trusts (REITs), or house flipping, real estate offers multiple avenues to build wealth.

However, real estate requires more active management than index funds. You need to consider the costs of property maintenance, vacancies, and market fluctuations. That said, when done right, real estate can be a powerful wealth-building tool within the FIRE strategy.

Dividend Stocks

Another popular investment option for those pursuing FIRE is dividend-paying stocks. These stocks provide regular payouts, typically quarterly, in addition to potential growth in stock value. For some, the goal is to build a portfolio that generates enough passive income through dividends to cover their living expenses, allowing them to live off the returns without needing to sell the underlying stocks.

While dividend stocks can provide a steady income, it's important to diversify. Relying too heavily on a handful of dividend stocks can expose you to risk if those companies reduce or eliminate their dividend payouts.

5. Creating a Sustainable Withdrawal Strategy

Once you've built up your FIRE portfolio, the next challenge is figuring out how to safely withdraw from it in a way that doesn't deplete your savings too quickly. This is where a sustainable withdrawal strategy comes into play.

The 4% Rule

As mentioned earlier, the 4% rule is a commonly used guideline in the FIRE community. It suggests that if you withdraw 4% of your total portfolio each year, adjusted for inflation, your money should last throughout your retirement. This rule is based on historical data showing that a diversified portfolio of stocks and bonds has, in most cases, been able to sustain such withdrawals over 30 years or more.

However, it's important to note that the 4% rule isn't a guarantee. Market conditions, inflation, and unexpected expenses can impact your portfolio. Some people opt for a more conservative withdrawal rate of 3-3.5% to add a cushion, especially if they're retiring very early and need their money to last 40 years or more.

Flexibility

The key to a successful withdrawal strategy is flexibility. You may need to adjust your spending in response to market downturns or changes in your lifestyle. Being willing to cut back during lean years or supplement your income with part-time work can help you weather economic storms and ensure your portfolio lasts as long as you need it to.

6. The Psychological Shift to FIRE

Achieving FIRE isn't just a financial transformation—it's also a major psychological one. As you approach financial independence, you'll need to shift your mindset from one of accumulation to one of sustainable living and purposeful spending.

Many people struggle with the idea of retiring early, not because of money, but because they haven't thought about how they want to spend their time. Without the structure of a job, it's easy to feel lost or unproductive. That's why it's crucial to have a clear vision of what you want your post-FIRE life to look like.

Do you want to travel the world? Volunteer? Start a passion project or business? Having a strong sense of purpose will keep you motivated and fulfilled once you reach FIRE.

In Summary

The FIRE movement is more than just a financial goal—it's about creating a life that gives you the freedom to choose how you spend your time. By focusing on aggressive saving, smart investing, and developing a clear vision for your post-FIRE life, you can achieve financial independence and retire early.

In the next chapter, we'll explore how to maintain financial independence and manage your wealth long-term. Once you've reached FIRE, the journey doesn't stop—maintaining it requires ongoing planning and flexibility to ensure your financial freedom lasts throughout your life.

Conclusion: Taking Control of Your Financial Future

Reaching the end of this book brings us to a crucial realization: financial independence isn't just a dream reserved for a select few; it's a realistic, attainable goal for anyone willing to make smart choices and commit to long-term planning. Throughout this journey, we've explored the foundations of personal finance, from budgeting and debt management to investing and wealth-building. These principles serve as your financial toolbox—equipping you with the skills and knowledge to take control of your financial destiny.

1. Your Financial Health is a Lifelong Journey

The path to financial independence is not a one-time achievement, but a lifelong journey. It's important to recognize that your financial needs, priorities, and goals will evolve over time, and so will your strategies. The habits you form today—like budgeting, saving, and investing—will serve as cornerstones for a stable financial future. But just as your personal life changes, so should your approach to managing your money.

Regularly reviewing your financial goals, adjusting your spending, and staying informed about economic trends will ensure that you remain on track to financial independence. Flexibility and resilience are key to maintaining long-term financial health.

2. Freedom Through Financial Independence

Financial independence isn't solely about accumulating wealth; it's about gaining the freedom to live life on your own terms. Whether that means retiring early, pursuing your passions, traveling the world, or simply having the peace of mind that you're financially secure—financial independence gives you the power to shape your future.

It's essential to remember that this freedom doesn't come solely from the money in your bank account, but from how you manage and optimize your resources. With discipline, consistency, and a clear vision of your goals, you can build a financial life that supports the lifestyle you've always dreamed of.

3. Stay Committed to Growth

Achieving financial independence requires a growth mindset—one that is open to learning, adapting, and continually improving. The world of finance is always changing, and staying informed and proactive will help you make the best decisions for your future. Educate yourself, seek out advice when needed, and remain humble about what you don't know.

Furthermore, don't be afraid to challenge your own assumptions and adjust your strategies as you gain new knowledge. Whether it's exploring new investment options, reevaluating your retirement plan, or finding new ways to save, staying open to growth will ensure that you keep progressing toward your goals.

4. Your Next Steps

The journey to financial independence begins now. Whether you're just starting with a budget or are already deeply involved in investing, the most important thing is to take action. Start by reviewing your current financial situation and setting realistic, actionable goals. Identify areas where you can improve—whether it's reducing debt, saving more aggressively, or learning about new investment opportunities.

Remember, the small decisions you make daily—like opting to save rather than spend, or learning a new skill to increase your income—compound over time, just like your investments. Keep these habits in place, and they will lead to significant financial rewards in the future.

5. Your Financial Independence, Your Life

At the heart of financial independence lies the idea that it's your life to design. Money is merely a tool to help you build the life you desire. It's important to keep sight of what truly matters—your values, relationships, health, and well-being. Financial success is only meaningful if it enhances these aspects of your life.

As you move forward, remember that financial independence is not an end in itself but a means to an enriched, fulfilling life. Define what success means for you, and align your financial goals with that vision. Every step you take from here brings you closer to financial freedom—and the ability to live life on your terms.

Final Thoughts

This book has covered the essential tools and strategies to master personal finance, but your journey doesn't stop here. Continue to educate yourself, seek new opportunities, and refine your financial goals. By maintaining discipline, consistency, and a clear focus on your long-term vision, you'll achieve the financial independence that opens the door to the life you've always wanted.

www.ingramcontent.com/pod-product-compliance
Lightning Source LLC
Chambersburg PA
CBHW071100240526
45471CB00016B/2205